Early Maths
Simple Multiplication

Multiplication is repeated addition.

For example:

2 multiplied by 5 = 2 + 2 + 2 + 2 + 2= 10
The number 2 is added 5 times. This is why multiplication is also called 'times'.

Let us look at some more examples:

5 x 3 = 5 + 5 + 5 = 15
7 x 2 = 7 + 7 = 14
5 x 6 = 5 + 5 + 5 + 5 + 5 + 5 = 30

The most common sign that denotes multiplication is 'x'. Sometimes people use an asterisk (*) sign or other symbols.

Here are some ways to indicate 4 multiplied by 7.

Sometimes in multiplication the variables are placed next to each other to indicate multiplication.

For example:

ab = a x b

Some rules for multiplication

Multiplying by 0 & 1

- When multiplying any number by 0, the answer is always 0.

For example:

1 x 0 = 0
0 x 12 = 0

84526 x 0 = 0
0 x 0.2 = 0

- When multiplying any number by 1, the answer is always the same as the number multiplied by 1.

For example:

1 x 12 = 12
1 x 9 = 9

2546 x 1 = 2546
1 x 0.2 = 0.2

Just like addition, the order of the numbers being multiplied does not matter. The answer will remain the same.

For example:

5 x 3 = 3 + 3 + 3 + 3 + 3 = 15
3 x 5 = 5 + 5 + 5 = 15

4 x 6 = 6 + 6 + 6 + 6 = 24
6 x 4 = 4 + 4 + 4 + 4 + 4 + 4 = 24

9 x 1 = 1 + 1 + 1 + 1 + 1 + 1 + 1 +1 + 1 = 9
1 x 9 = 9

Here are the multiplication tables from 1-12. Memorize them all.

The multiplication table, also called the times table includes multiplications between the

1x

1 x 1 = 1
1 x 2 = 2
1 x 3 = 3
1 x 4 = 4
1 x 5 = 5
1 x 6 = 6
1 x 7 = 7
1 x 8 = 8
1 x 9 = 9
1 x 10 = 10

2x

2 x 1 = 2
2 x 2 = 4
2 x 3 = 6
2 x 4 = 8
2 x 5 = 10
2 x 6 = 12
2 x 7 = 14
2 x 8 = 16
2 x 9 = 18
2 x 10 = 20

3 x 1 = 3
3 x 2 = 6
3 x 3 = 9
3 x 4 = 12
3 x 5 = 15
3 x 6 = 18
3 x 7 = 21
3 x 8 = 24
3 x 9 = 27
3 x 10 = 30

7 x 1 = 7
7 x 2 = 14
7 x 3 = 21
7 x 4 = 28
7 x 5 = 35
7 x 6 = 42
7 x 7 = 49
7 x 8 = 56
7 x 9 = 63
7 x 10 = 70

8 x 1 = 8
8 x 2 = 16
8 x 3 = 24
8 x 4 = 32
8 x 5 = 40
8 x 6 = 48
8 x 7 = 56
8 x 8 = 64
8 x 9 = 72
8 x 10 = 80

9 x 1 = 9
9 x 2 = 18
9 x 3 = 27
9 x 4 = 36
9 x 5 = 45
9 x 6 = 54
9 x 7 = 63
9 x 8 = 72
9 x 9 = 81
9 x 10 = 90

numbers. It is very useful to memorise these tables. It helps to solve harder problems faster. Solving multiplication problems will become easier if you know these numbers by heart.

4x

4 x 1 = 4
4 x 2 = 8
4 x 3 = 12
4 x 4 = 16
4 x 5 = 20
4 x 6 = 24
4 x 7 = 28
4 x 8 = 32
4 x 9 = 36
4 x 10 = 40

5x

5 x 1 = 5
5 x 2 = 10
5 x 3 = 15
5 x 4 = 20
5 x 5 = 25
5 x 6 = 30
5 x 7 = 35
5 x 8 = 40
5 x 9 = 45
5 x 10 = 50

6x

6 x 1 = 6
6 x 2 = 12
6 x 3 = 18
6 x 4 = 24
6 x 5 = 30
6 x 6 = 36
6 x 7 = 42
6 x 8 = 48
6 x 9 = 54
6 x 10 = 60

10x

10 x 1 = 10
10 x 2 = 20
10 x 3 = 30
10 x 4 = 40
10 x 5 = 50
10 x 6 = 60
10 x 7 = 70
10 x 8 = 80
10 x 9 = 90
10 x 10 = 100

11 x 1 = 11
11 x 2 = 22
11 x 3 = 33
11 x 4 = 44
11 x 5 = 55
11 x 6 = 66
11 x 7 = 77
11 x 8 = 88
11 x 9 = 99
11 x 10 = 110

12 x 1 = 12
12 x 2 = 24
12 x 3 = 36
12 x 4 = 48
12 x 5 = 60
12 x 6 = 72
12 x 7 = 84
12 x 8 = 96
12 x 9 = 108
12 x 10 = 120

Multiply the numbers and find the answers.

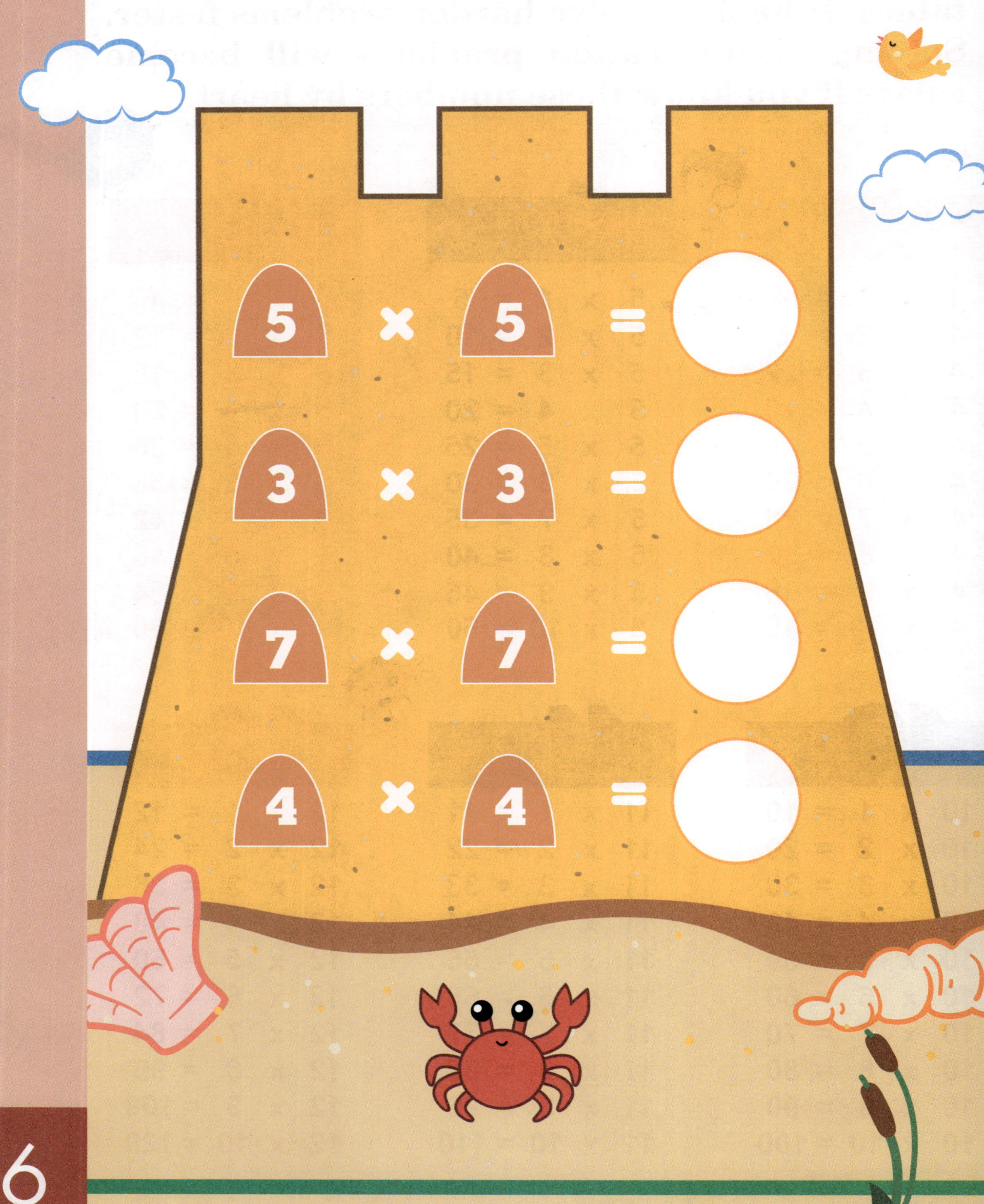

7 × 6 =

8 × 4 =

5 × 9 =

3 × 6 =

Count each set of objects and multiply.

Count, multiply and match with correct answer.

10

16

6

Multiply and colour according to the given number key

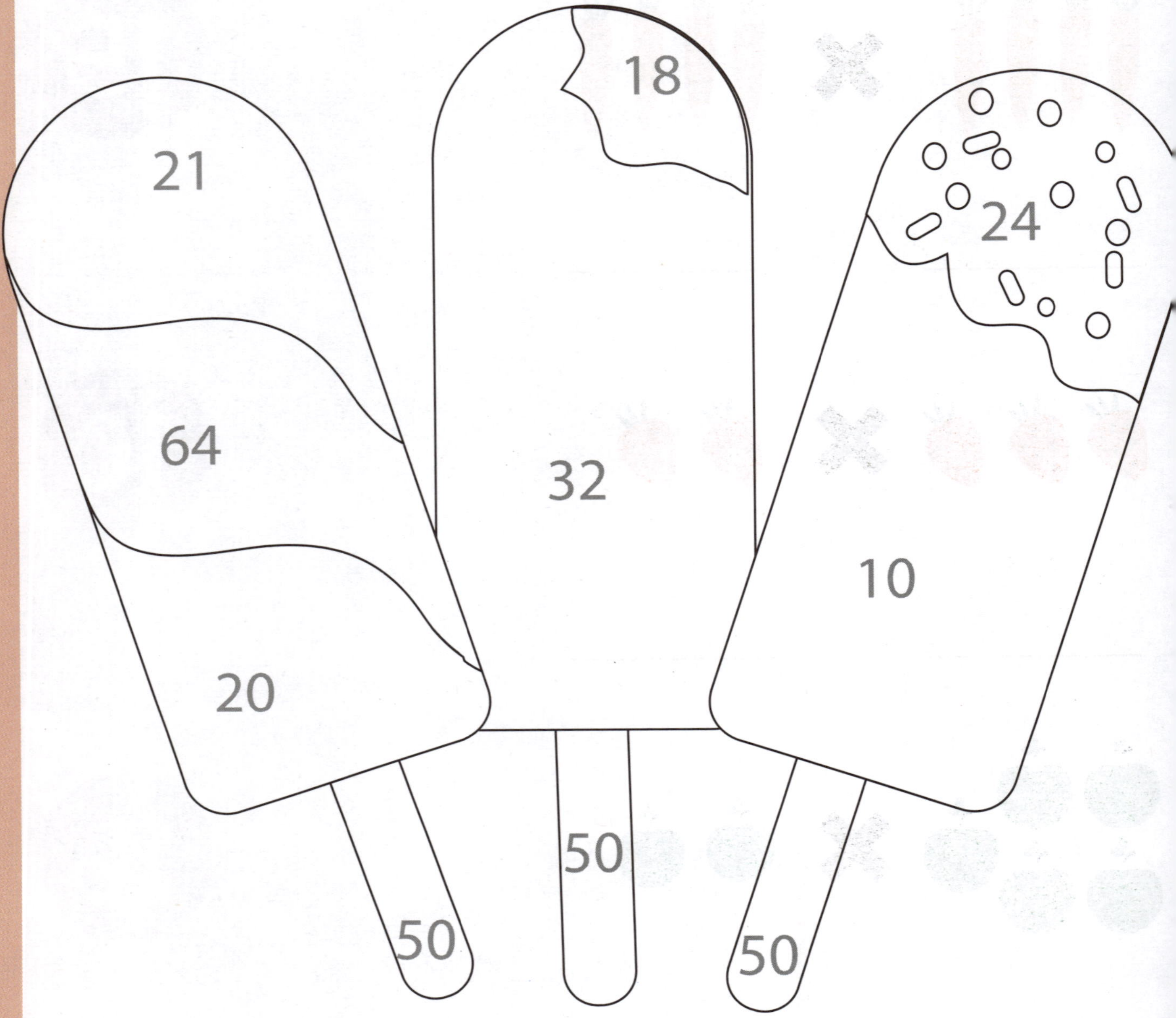

18

21

24

64

32

10

20

50

50

50

Complete the table of 5.

5 × 1 = ☐

5 × 2 = ☐

5 × 3 = ☐

5 × 4 = ☐

5 × 5 = ☐

5 × 6 = ☐

5 × 7 = ☐

5 × 8 = ☐

5 × 9 = ☐

5 × 10 = ☐

Multiply and find the answer.

6 × 1 = ☐

5 × 4 = ☐

2 × 8 = ☐

7 × 3 = ☐

9 × 5 = ☐

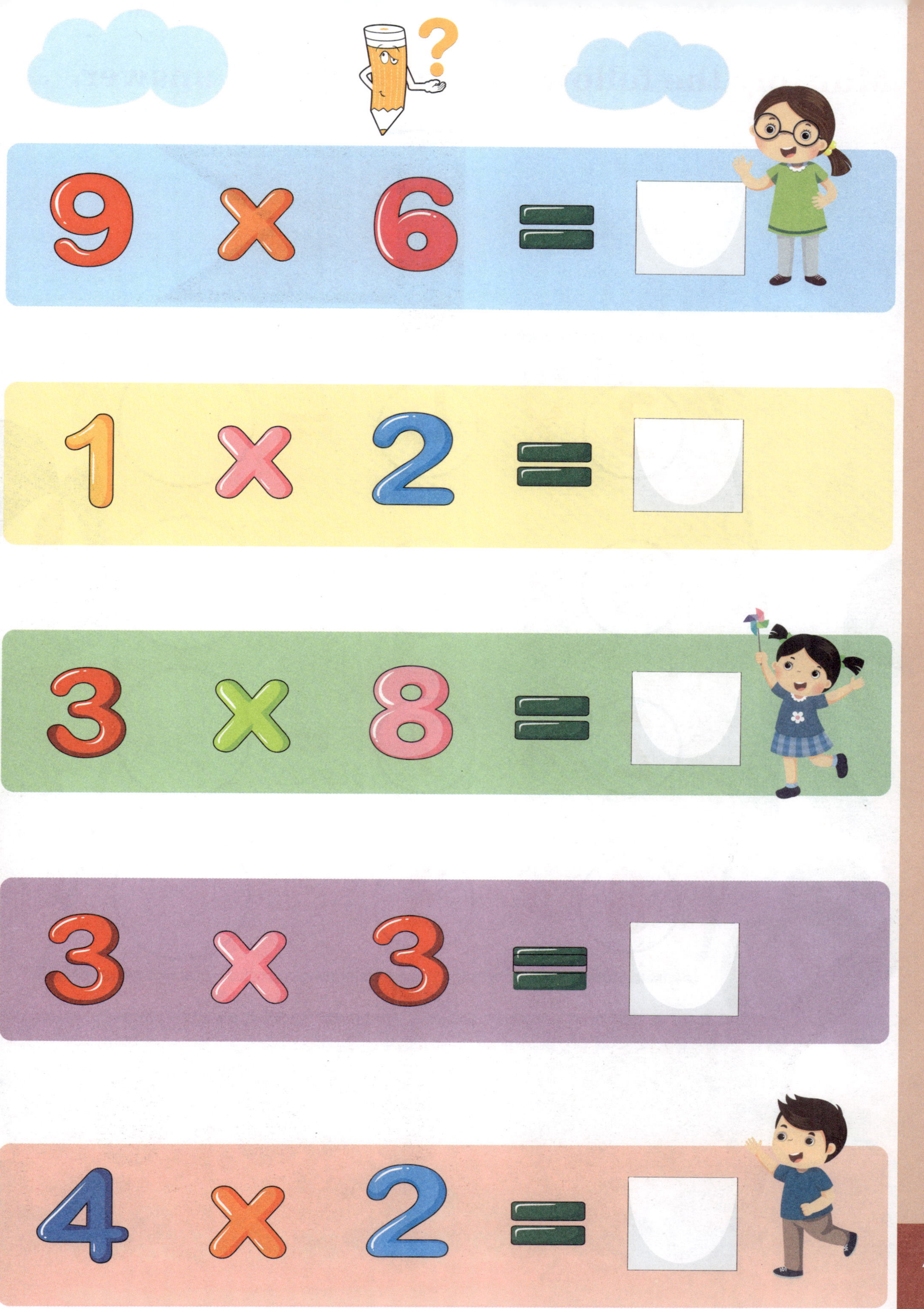
9 × 6 =
1 × 2 =
3 × 8 =
3 × 3 =
4 × 2 =

Multiply the following and write the answer.

7 × 9 =
5 × 1 =
4 × 8 =
6 × 6 =

Count each set of objects and multiply to find the answer.

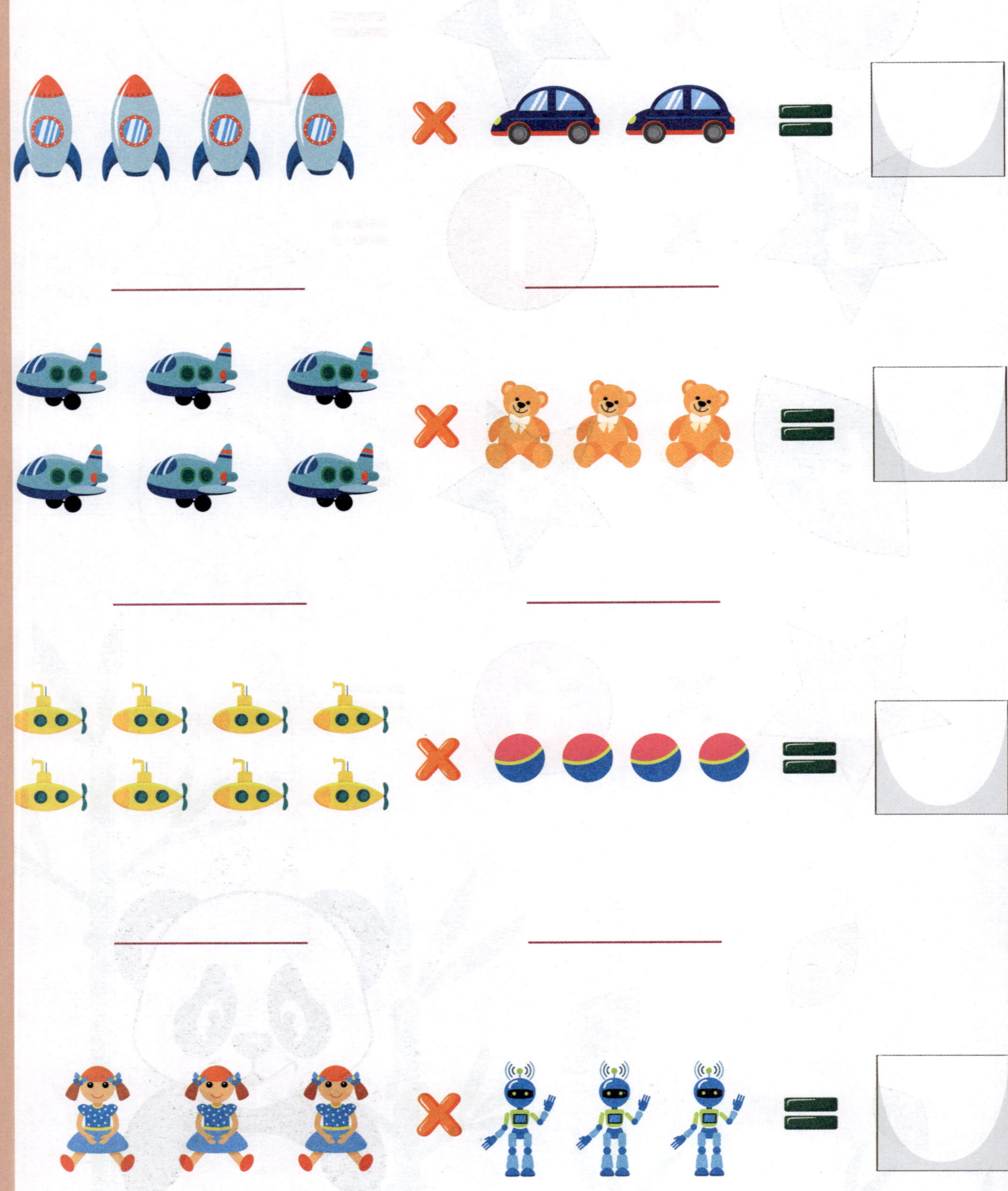

Complete the table of 3.

3 × 1 = ______

3 × 2 = ______

3 × 3 = ______

3 × 4 = ______

3 × 5 = ______

3 × 6 = ______

3 × 7 = ______

3 × 8 = ______

3 × 9 = ______

3 × 10 = ______

Multiply and solve the problem.

4 × 5 =

7 × 7 =

6 × 6 =

Fill in the missing numbers and solve the puzzle.

Let us use multiplication to find some answers in our daily life.

- If there are 4 balls in 1 box – 4 x 1 = 4

  How many balls will be there in 4 boxes?

4 x 4 =_____

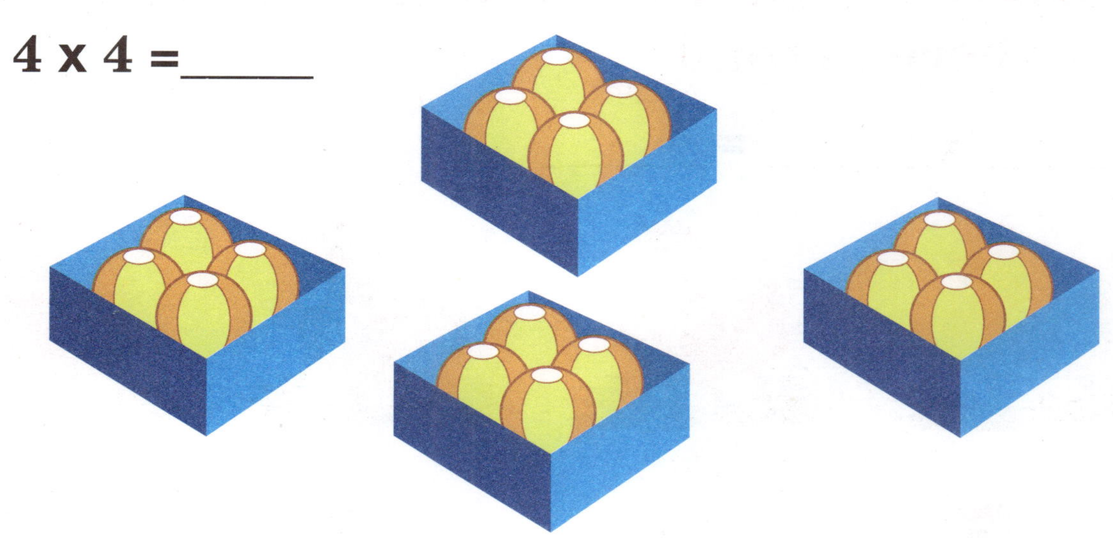

- If there are 5 balls in one box, how many balls are there in 5 boxes?

5 x 5 = _______

- **1 hen lays 10 eggs at a time. How many eggs do 8 hens lay?**

_______ x _______ = _______

- **9 baskets have 7 eggs each. How many eggs are there in total?**

_______ x _______ = _______

- **If 1 packet has 10 candies, how many candies are there if you buy 9 packets?**

_______ x _______ = _______

- **Cyril gives 2 candy canes to each of his friends. If he has 4 friends, how many candy canes did he have in total?**

_______ x _______ = _______

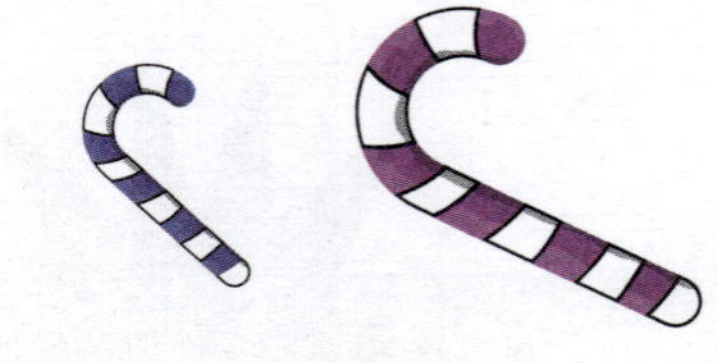

- A cat drinks 2 bowls of milk in a day. How many bowls of milk does he drink in 5 days?

_____ x _____ = _____

- If a cat drinks 3 bowls of milk in a day, how many bowls of milk does he drink in 7 days?

_____ x _____ = _____

- 1 book costs $8. How much do 6 books cost?

$_____ x $_____ = $_____

- A pen costs $2. What is the cost of 7 such pens?

$_____ x $_____ = $_____

If there are 10 biscuits in a jar, how many biscuits will be there in:

9 jars: ______ x ______ = ______

4 jars: ______ x ______ = ______

5 jars: ______ x ______ = ______

7 jars: ______ x ______ = ______

One classroom has 8 benches, how many benches do 6 classrooms have?

______ x ______ = ______

There are 4 classrooms on 1 floor. How many classrooms are there if there are 4 floors?

______ x ______ = ______

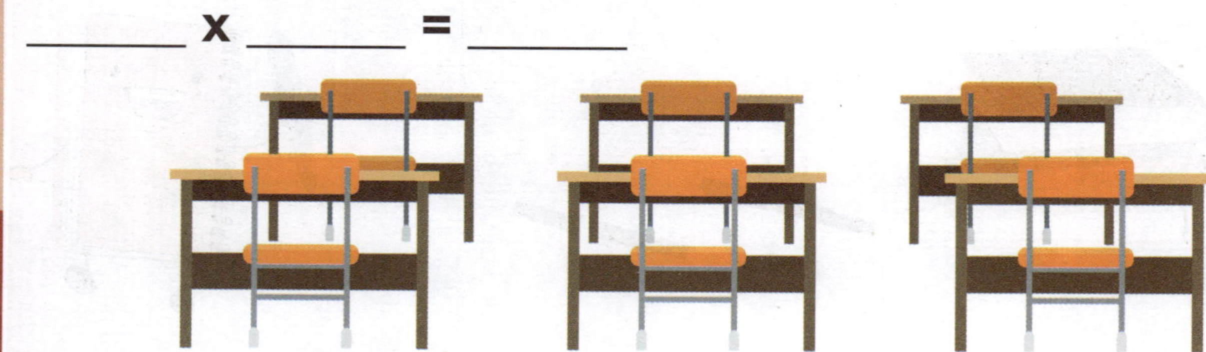

Multiply in groups.

- There are 9 roses in 5 parks. How many roses are there in total?

_______ x _______ = _______

- There are 6 tulips in 3 parks. How many tulips are there in total?

_______ x _______ = _______

- There are 10 sunflowers in 6 parks. How many sunflowers are there in total?

_______ x _______ = _______

- There are 8 daisies in 4 parks. How many daisies are there in total?

_______ x _______ = _______

- If there are 8 points in 1 octagon, how many points are there in 8 octagons?

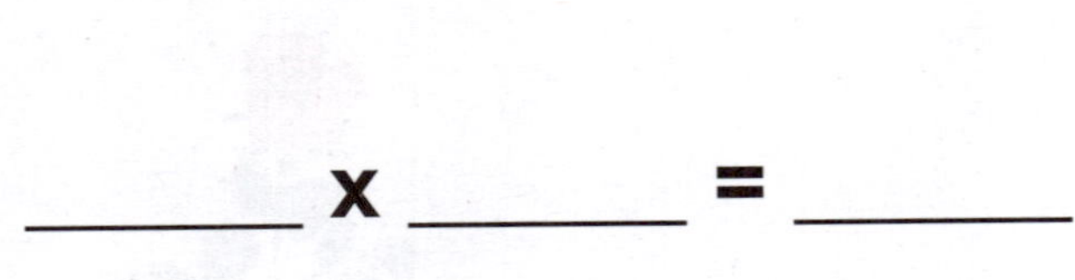

_______ x _______ = _______

- If there are 6 points in 1 hexagon, how many points are there in 2 hexagons?

_______ x _______ = _______

- If there are 5 points in 1 star, how many points are there in 7 stars?

_______ x _______ = _______

- If there are 3 points in a triangle, how many points are there in 6 triangles?

_______ x _______ = _______

- **If there are 5 points in a pentagon, how many points are there in 9 pentagons?**

______ x ______ = ______

- **If there are 7 points in a heptagon, how many points are there in 7 heptagons?**

______ x ______ = ______

- **If there are 4 points in a square, how many points are there in 4 squares?**

______ x ______ = ______

- **If there no points in a circle, how any points are there in 10 circles?**

______ x ______ = ______

Here are some tips and tricks that will help with multiplication. Use these to solve the problems quickly.

Use multiples to find the answer:

Multiples of a number are formed by multiplying it with other numbers like 1,2,3 and so on. Multiples of 2 are- 2, 4, 6, 8 etc.

Let us say that you cannot remember what 6 x 7 is, but you can remember that 6 x 5 = 30. Now you can just keep on adding 6's to 30: 30 + 6 = 36, 36 + 6 = 42, therefore 6 x 7 = 42.

When multiplying by the number:

2 - the answer will always be an even number.

5 - The answer will always end in 0 or 5. 5 x 5 = 25, 5 x 8=40

9 - In the 9 times table, the sum of the digits of each product is equal to nine.
9x2= 18 (1+8= 9), 9x3= 27 (2+7= 9)

ending in 0 - Just put a zero behind the other number. With 100 put two zeros. 10 x 3 = 30, 100 x 3 = 300

11 - When multiplying 11 by numbers less than 10, just write the number twice in the answer. For example, 7 x 11 = 77, 8 x 11 = 88

If 1 monkey eats 6 bananas, how many bananas will be eaten by 9 monkeys?

☐ x ☐ = ☐

A rabbit has 8 packs of 7 carrots. How many carrots are there in total?

☐ x ☐ = ☐

A bird has 2 wings. How many wings do 4 birds have?

☐ x ☐ = ☐

Now colour the butterfly according to the given number key.

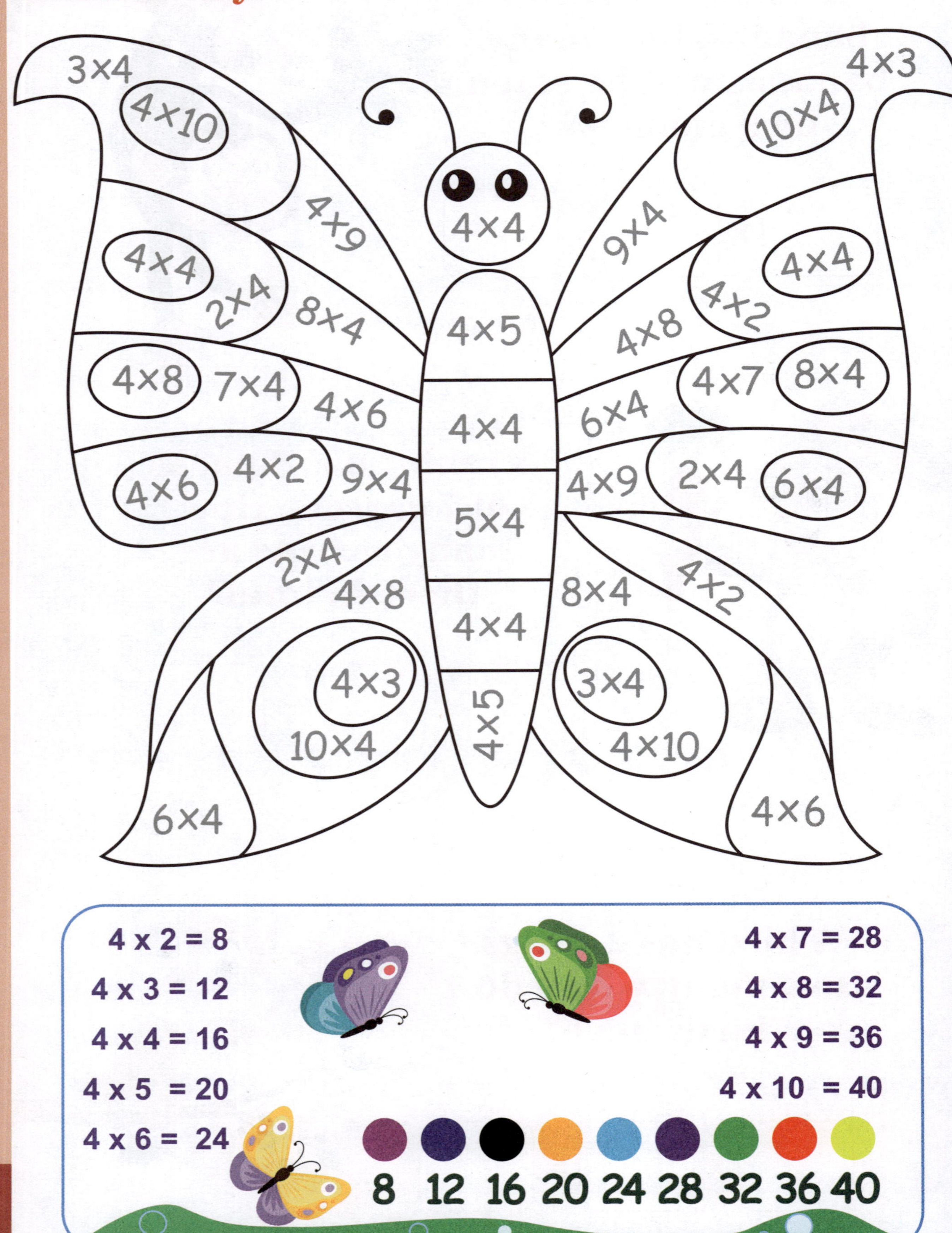

Complete the table of 7.

7 × 1 = ☐

7 × 2 = ☐

7 × 3 = ☐

7 × 4 = ☐

7 × 5 = ☐

7 × 6 = ☐

7 × 7 = ☐

7 × 8 = ☐

7 × 9 = ☐

7 × 10 = ☐

Let us make multiplication easier. Sometimes, it is easier to break apart numbers and then add the two results to solve multiplication problems.

For example:

14 x 12 = ?

You may not have memorized 14 x 12, but you should know 7 x 12 from the times table. So,

(2 x 7 x 12) = 2 x 84 = 84 + 84 = 168

Let us look at another example.

42 x 6 = ?

In this case we know 4 x 6 and 2 x 6.

Now break the problem according to the place values:

42 x 6

= (10 x 4 x 6) + (2 x 6)

= (10 x 24) + 12

= 240 + 12

= 252

Solve the problems using this method.

Complete the table of 10.

10 × 1 = ☐

10 × 2 = ☐

10 × 3 = ☐

10 × 4 = ☐

10 × 5 = ☐

10 × 6 = ☐

10 × 7 = ☐

10 × 8 = ☐

10 × 9 = ☐

10 × 10 = ☐

Multiply the number of objects with the number and write the answer.

× 17 =

× 16 =

× 13 =

× 15 =

$\times$ 14 =

$\times$ 17 =

$\times$ 12 =

$\times$ 11 =

Multiply and write the answer.

 ×  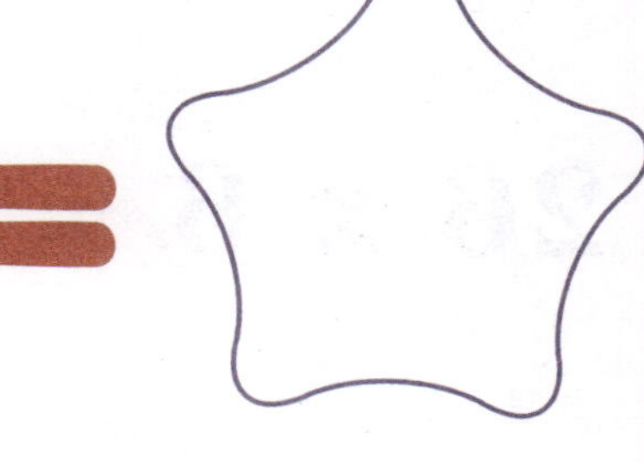

3 =

 ×  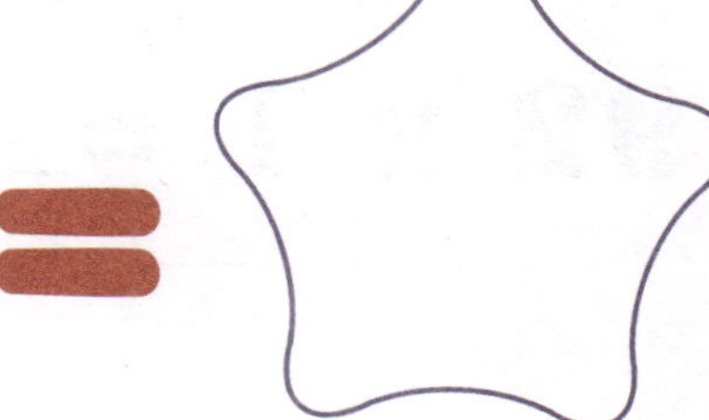

5 =

  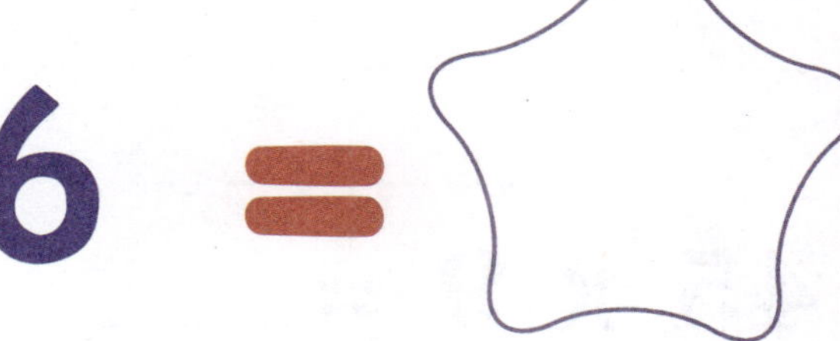

× 6 =

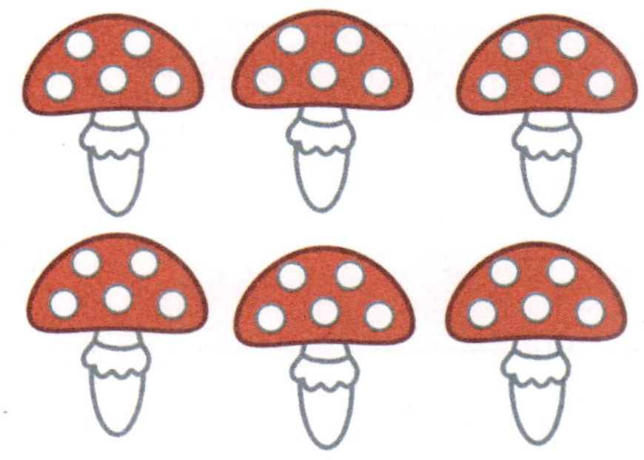  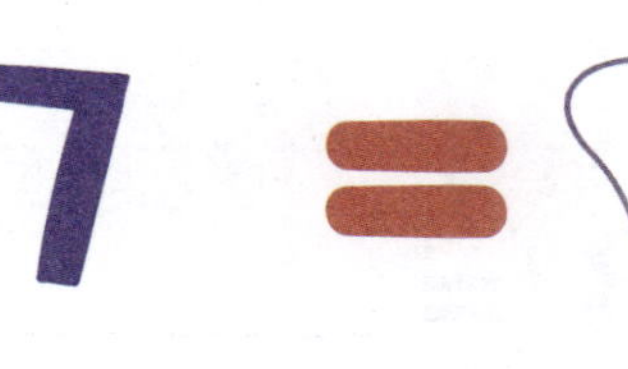 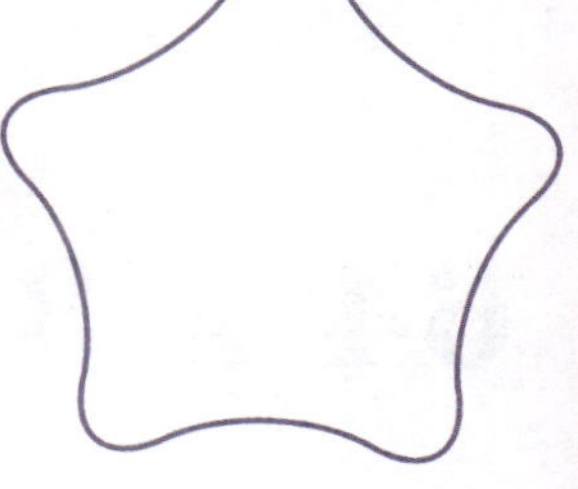

× 7 =

Solve the multiplication problems using the break apart method.

26 x 6 = ____________________

34 x 2 = ____________________

92 x 1 = ____________________

71 x 8 = ____________________

55 x 5 = ____________________

45 x 9 = ____________________

12 x 7 = ____________________

64 x 3 = ____________________

48 x 8 = ______________________

67 x 6 = ______________________

18 x 5 = ______________________

75 x 3 = ______________________

94 x 1 = ______________________

82 x 7 = ______________________

41 x 8 = ______________________

20 x 6 = ______________________

Match the caps and colour them accordingly.

Solve the word problems.

If 1 dozen bananas = 12 bananas, how many bananas will be there in 12 dozen?

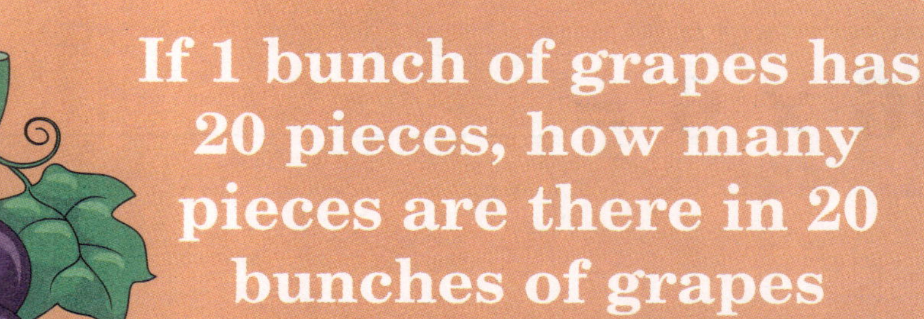

If 1 bunch of grapes has 20 pieces, how many pieces are there in 20 bunches of grapes

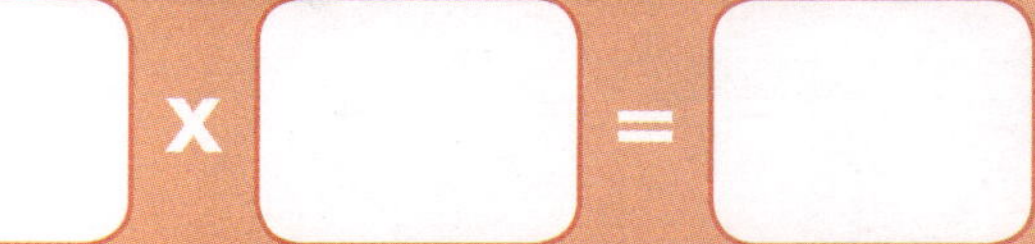

If there are 10 oranges in a basket, how many oranges are there in 16 baskets?

Multiply and find the answer.

35 x 7 = ______________________

40 x 6 = ______________________

74 x 2 = ______________________

96 x 6 = ______________________

52 x 3 = ______________________

16 x 8 = ______________________

66 x 7 = ______________________

73 x 6 = ______________________

68 x 2 = ______________________

52 x 3 = ______________________

16 x 6 = ______________________

85 x 1 = ______________________

19 x 6 = ______________________

15 x 5 = ______________________

33 x 5 = ______________________

21 x 8 = ______________________

Multiply and use the colour key to colour the flowers.

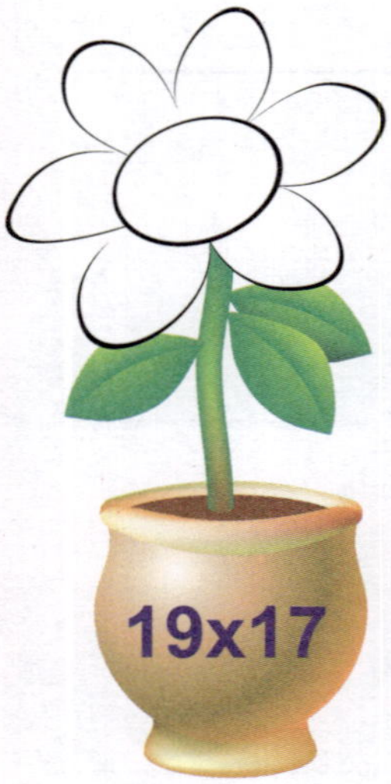

19x17 19x12 19x18 19x15

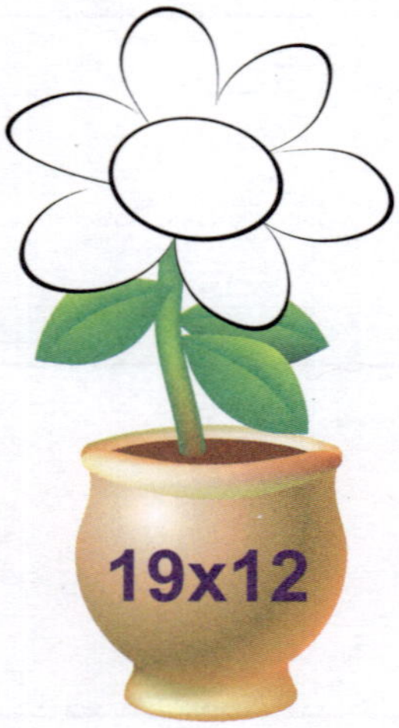

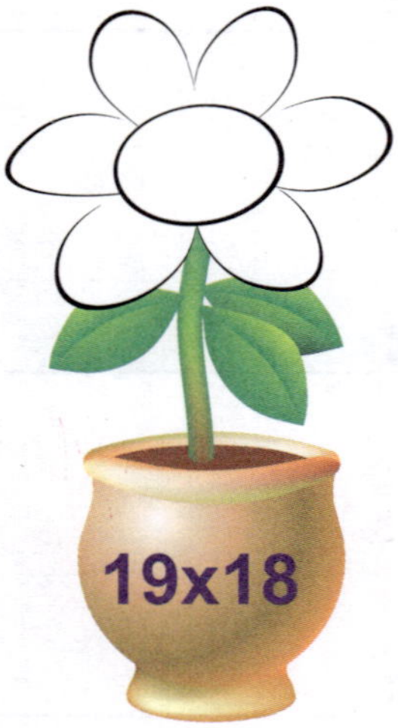

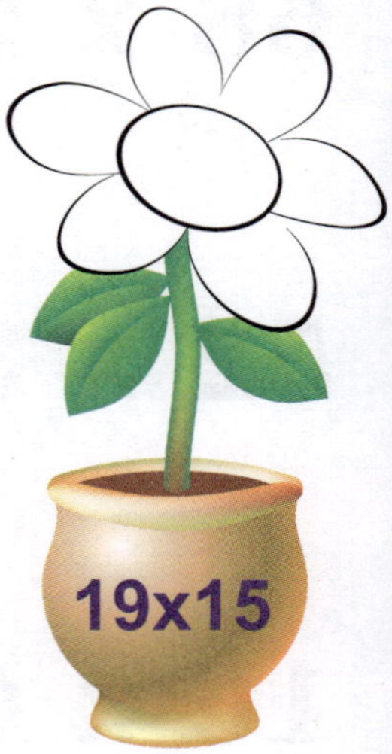

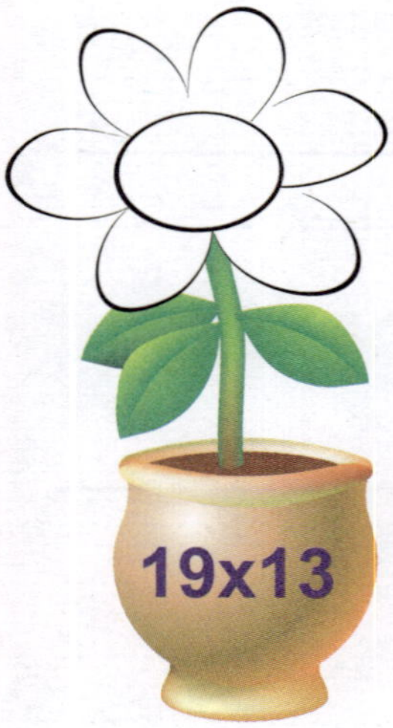

19x13 19x19 19x16 19x14

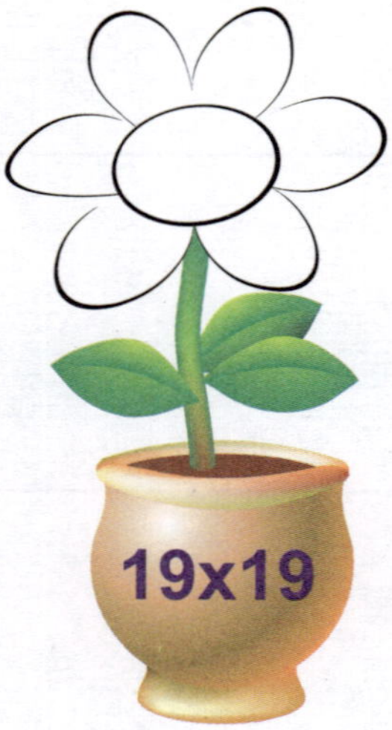

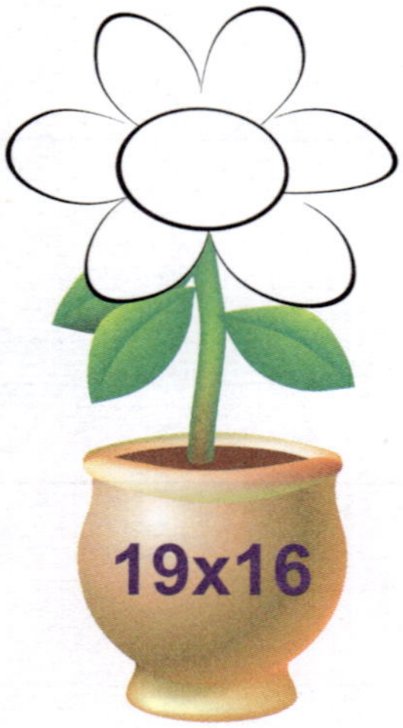

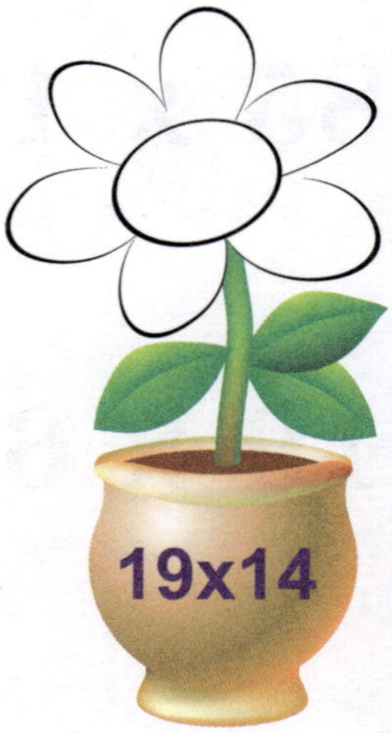

Solve the word problems.

There are 13 balloons in 1 bunch. If there are 10 bunches in total, what is the total number of balloons?

If there 11 apples on 1 tree, how many apples are on 15 trees?

If a flower bouquet has 29 flowers, how many flowers are there in 18 bouquets?

Long multiplication is a method used to solve multiplication problems with large numbers. Long multiplication is easy, especially if you know the multiplication table by heart. Follow the given steps to learn long multiplication.

1. Write down the numbers on top of each other. Align the numbers on the right. (Line up the right-most number)

For example: 612 x 24 = ?

2. Now start multiplying. Begin with the units place in the bottom number. This is the 4 in 24. Multiply 4 x 612 and write it down under the line.

3. Now multiply by the next number in the tens place, 2.

Place a zero in the units place before multiplying.

4. Now add up the rows of numbers to get the answer.

Solve the following problems using the long multiplication method.

$$\begin{array}{r} 842 \\ \times \ 39 \\ \hline \end{array}$$

$$\begin{array}{r} 584 \\ \times \ 85 \\ \hline \end{array}$$

$$\begin{array}{r} 985 \\ \times \ 74 \\ \hline \end{array}$$

$$\begin{array}{r} 440 \\ \times \ 64 \\ \hline \end{array}$$

$$\begin{array}{r} 984 \\ \times \ 95 \\ \hline \end{array}$$

$$\begin{array}{r} 473 \\ \times \ 80 \\ \hline \end{array}$$

$$\begin{array}{r} 942 \\ \times \ 58 \\ \hline \end{array}$$

$$\begin{array}{r} 839 \\ \times \ 87 \\ \hline \end{array}$$

$$\begin{array}{r} 585 \\ \times \ 51 \\ \hline \end{array}$$

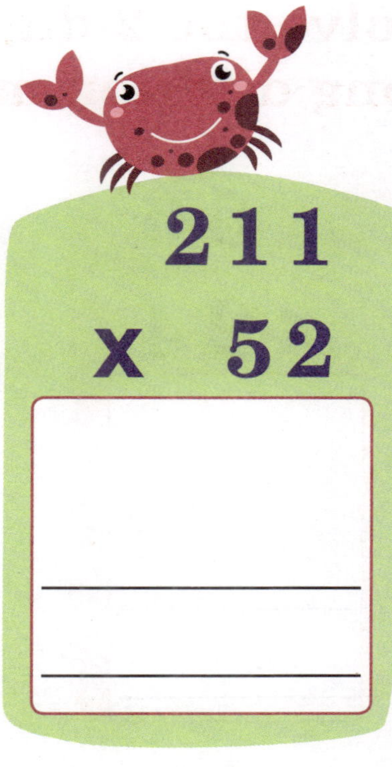

372	909	211
x 36	x 80	x 52

962	490	807
x 35	x 88	x 41

653	213	944
x 39	x 51	x 84

Solve the 2-digit multiplication problems using long division method.

56 x 24	78 x 42	93 x 50
12 x 10	34 x 59	67 x 74
25 x 39	45 x 92	83 x 64

96 x85	37 x23	58 x13
19 x35	48 x62	64 x98
10 x54	25 x12	15 x15

The rules for long division remain the same for 3-digit and 4-digit problems. Look at the following example.

5127 x 4265 = ?

Look carefully at the added zeroes in blue according to the place values. The number carried at the top is written in red.

1.

```
     13
   5127
x  4265
-------
  25635
```

2.

```
      14
    5127
x   4265
--------
   25635
  307620
```

3.

```
       1
    5127
x   4265
--------
   25635
  307620
 1025400
```

4.

```
       12
     5127
x    4265
---------
    25635
   307620
  1025400
 20508000
```

5.

```
       12
     5127
x    4265
---------
    25635
   307620
  1025400
 20508000
---------
 21866655
```

Solve the following 3-digit problems.

Follow the rules for numbers ending in zero and solve the following multiplication problems.

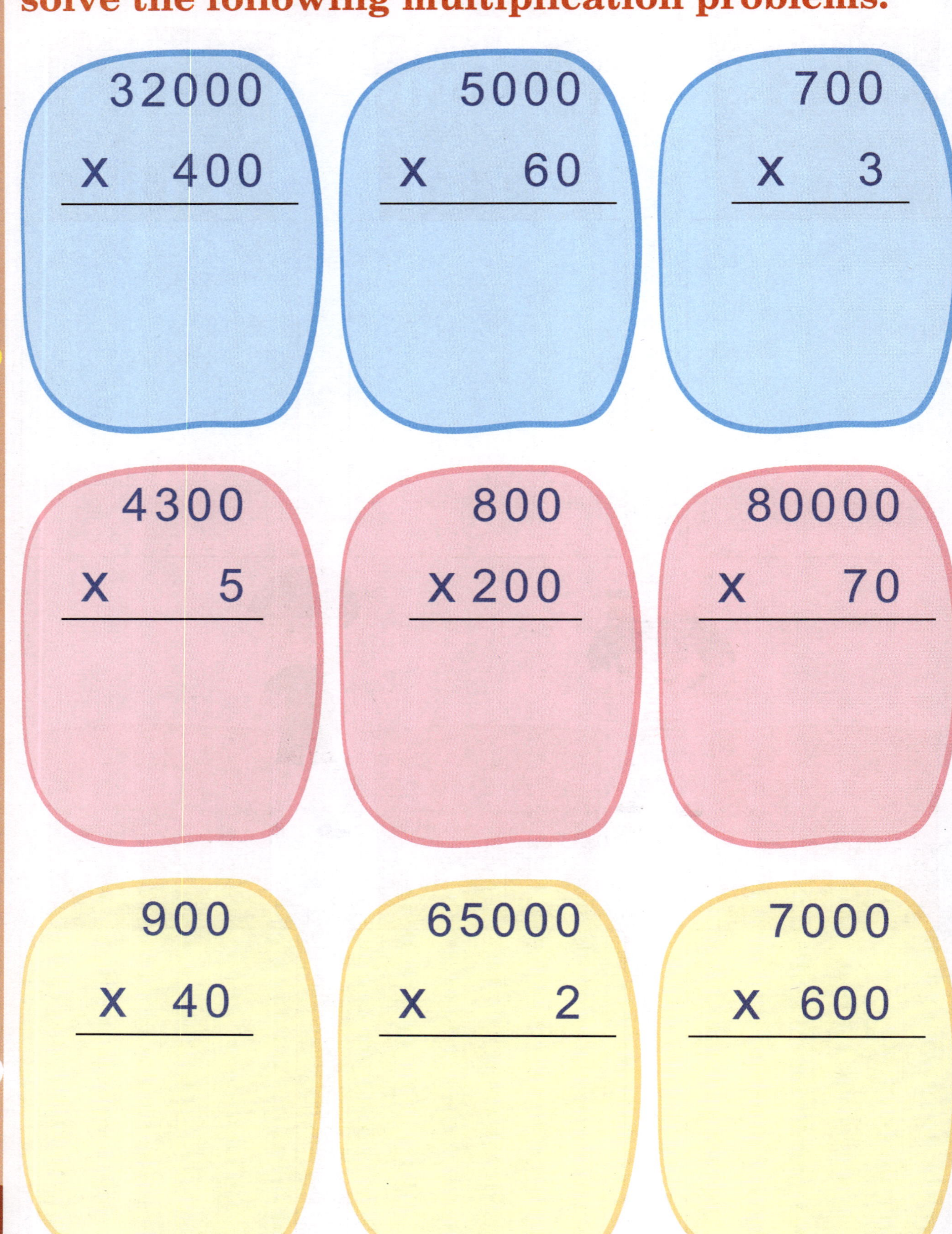

20000 x 30	3200 x 100	600 x 9
6000 x 8	500 x 70	80000 x 900
2500 x 40	10000 x 800	8400 x 2

Multiply 4-digit or 5-digit with 2-digit numbers and find the answers.

12492 x 45	6192 x 36	53476 x 77
8104 x 92	73438 x 81	2130 x 62
92603 x 43	5142 x 17	74267 x 38

4201 x 29	6084 x 70	27379 x 83
19892 x 65	35274 x 26	7483 x 48
2367 x 56	61120 x 28	78276 x 92

Solve the problems by multiplying 4 or 5-digit by 3-digit numbers.

$$\begin{array}{r} 63210 \\ \times \quad 725 \\ \hline \end{array}$$

$$\begin{array}{r} 41453 \\ \times \quad 346 \\ \hline \end{array}$$

$$\begin{array}{r} 7579 \\ \times \quad 189 \\ \hline \end{array}$$

$$\begin{array}{r} 1617 \\ \times \quad 618 \\ \hline \end{array}$$

$$\begin{array}{r} 87312 \\ \times \quad 477 \\ \hline \end{array}$$

$$\begin{array}{r} 59216 \\ \times \quad 831 \\ \hline \end{array}$$

$$\begin{array}{r} 28371 \\ \times \quad 505 \\ \hline \end{array}$$

$$\begin{array}{r} 3875 \\ \times \quad 267 \\ \hline \end{array}$$

$$\begin{array}{r} 92383 \\ \times \quad 738 \\ \hline \end{array}$$

7543	53990	6084
x 942	x 376	x 163

2314	49190	8635
x 648	x 924	x 567

6890	8765	2525
x 156	x 200	x 150

Solve the following multiplication problems with large numbers.

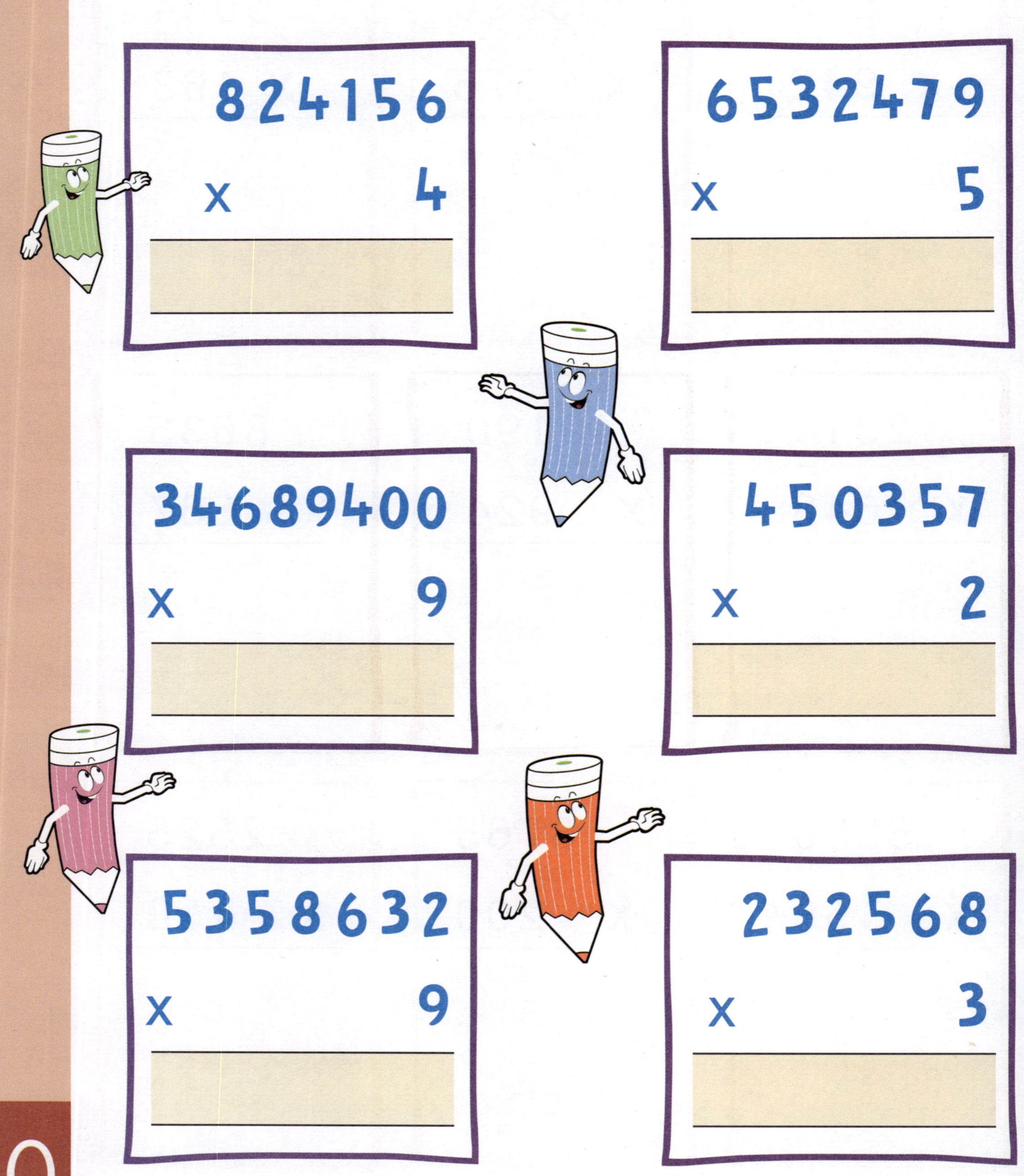

3578511
x 6

7632426
x 7

9365068
x 4

656368
x 9

3578903
x 5

167638
x 4

Multiply large numbers by 2-digit numbers.

340542
x 35

67673
x 94

923461
x 55

749184
x 37

Multiply and solve the word problems.

- If on an average a factory produces 28,800 bottles of juice in a day, how many bottles will it produce in 30 days?

____

- An apple tree in an orchard gives an average of 52 apples. If the orchard has 1,568 trees, how many apples in all can be found in the orchard?

____

- A car company sells 25,000 cars in a month. How many cars does it sell in 12 months?

____